MW01385426

Tree

A girl's journey to love

Denise Dauphine

This story is a journey of love: love of self, love of life, love of the light within.

For Linds
Who's love I cherish, who's light shines brightly,
who's laughter is music to my soul.
Love you more than you think I do

One fine day a girl was walking.
No one was with her, no one was talking.

She happened to look down and what did she see? A little green shoot, the beginnings of tree.

The girl felt delighted by this tiny shoot, so delicate and fragile it seemed to be.

What if she nourished
and loved that little tree?
Could her breath and her strength and
her love be the key?

To help it grow strong and steady,
such a beautiful sight,
that adults would admire,
and cause children delight.

So the girl made a promise
to herself and the tree.
If she gave of herself to this tree
everyday it surely would grow,
in the most lovely of ways.

Its roots so secure way down in the earth.
Its trunk strong and solid, a mighty fine girth.
Its branches spread wide
looking down from above.

Then the tree would be able
to feel the girl's love,
and in turn the tree
could give back to the girl.

The love that was given could then start to swirl.
Around and around, up high then down low,
so those who could feel it, could help it to grow.

Then before the girl knew it,
the tree and the love
had grown in ways that she
had never dreamed of.

All she had to do was stand strong and stand tall,
and if she believed, she'd feel no fear at all.
You see... the tree was the girl
and the girl was the tree,
and all of her love had set the girl free.

To become,
To love,
Tree.

The End

Coming Next: **Headstand**

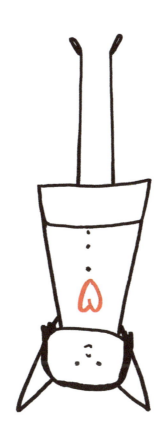

Tree: A girl's journey to love

ISBN: 9781939739155

Printed in the United States of America

www.fortheloveofallbeings.com